COMPOSER SHOWCASE
HAL LEONARD
STUDENT PIANO LIBRARY

Little Blues Concerto

PIANO SOLO WITH PIANO ACCOMPANIMENT

BY EUGÉNIE ROCHEROLLE

ISBN 978-1-4950-1312-6

HAL•LEONARD®
CORPORATION
7777 W. BLUEMOUND RD. P.O. BOX 13819 MILWAUKEE, WI 53213

In Australia Contact:
Hal Leonard Australia Pty. Ltd.
4 Lentara Court
Cheltenham, Victoria, 3192 Australia
Email: ausadmin@halleonard.com.au

Visit Hal Leonard Online at
www.halleonard.com

Little Blues Concerto
Piano Solo with Piano Accompaniment

By Eugénie Rocherolle

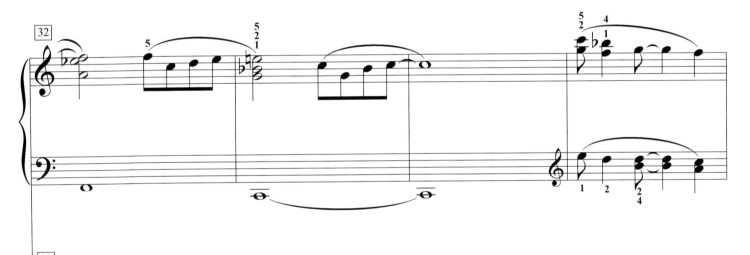

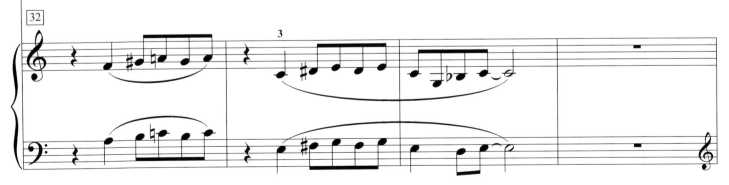

COMPOSER SHOWCASE
HAL LEONARD
STUDENT PIANO LIBRARY

TWO PIANOS, FOUR HANDS – EARLY INTERMEDIATE LEVEL

Little Blues Concerto

PIANO SOLO WITH PIANO ACCOMPANIMENT

BY EUGÉNIE ROCHEROLLE

HAL•LEONARD®
CORPORATION

7777 W. BLUEMOUND RD. P.O. BOX 13819 MILWAUKEE, WI 53213

HL00142801

Little Blues Concerto
Piano Solo with Piano Accompaniment

By Eugénie Rocherolle

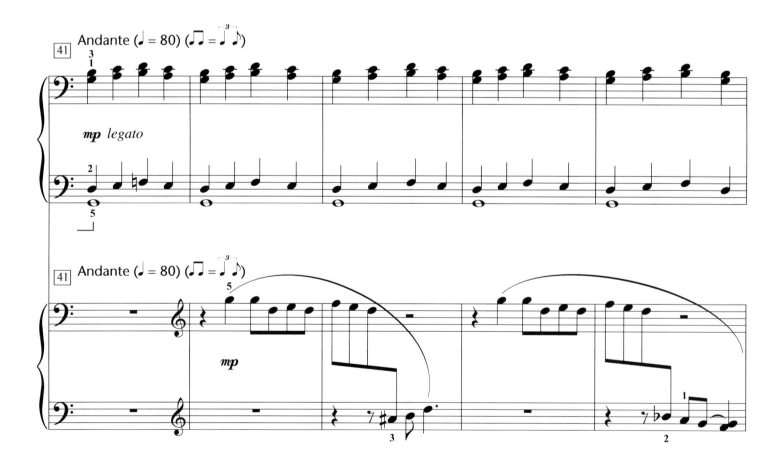

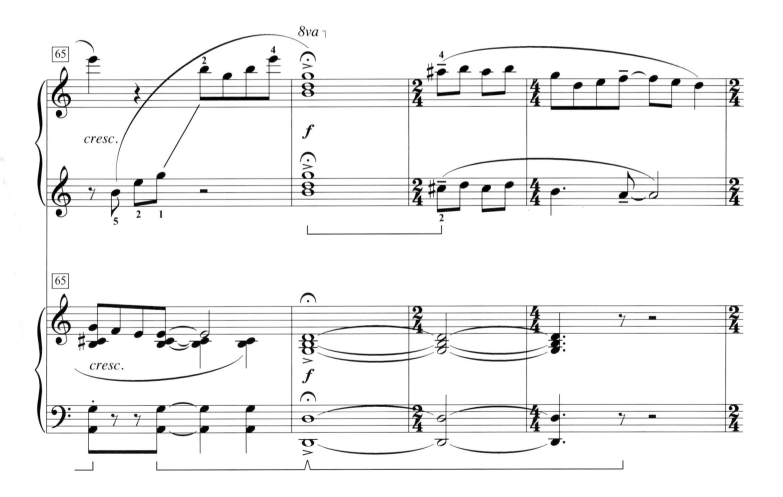

subito *mp*   *cresc. poco a poco*

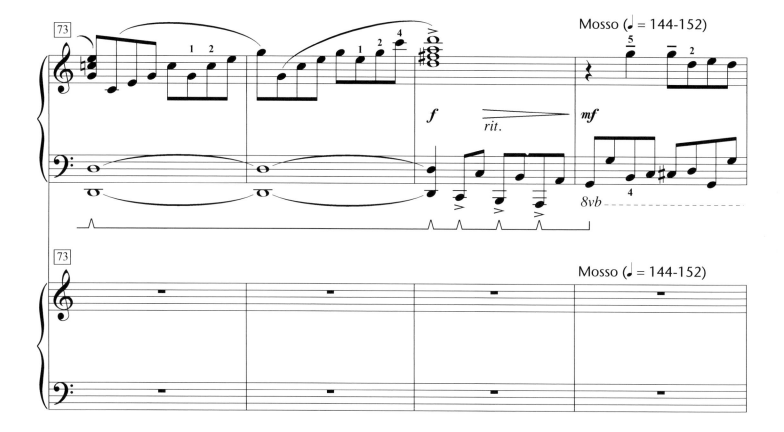

Mosso (♩ = 144-152)

f   *rit.*   *mf*

8vb

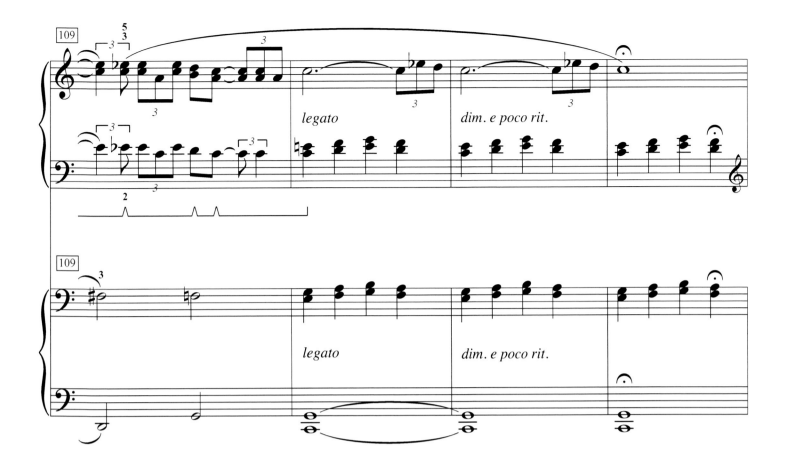

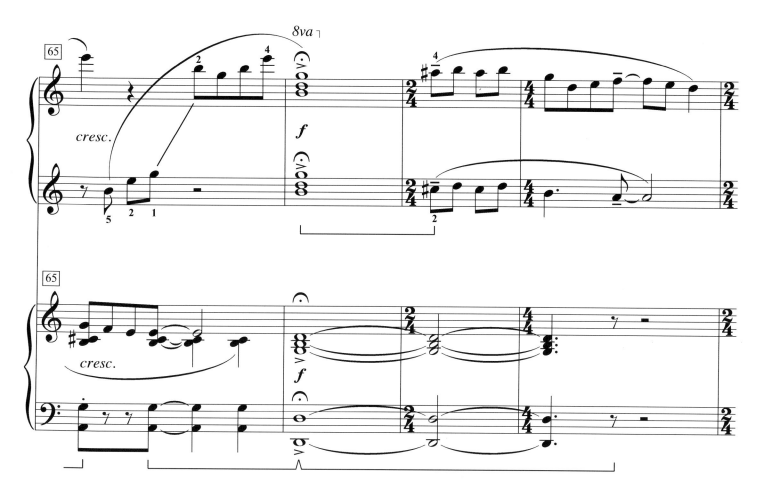

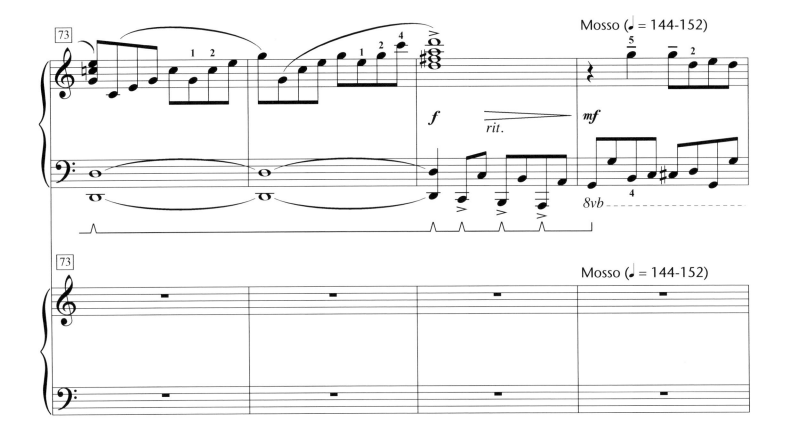

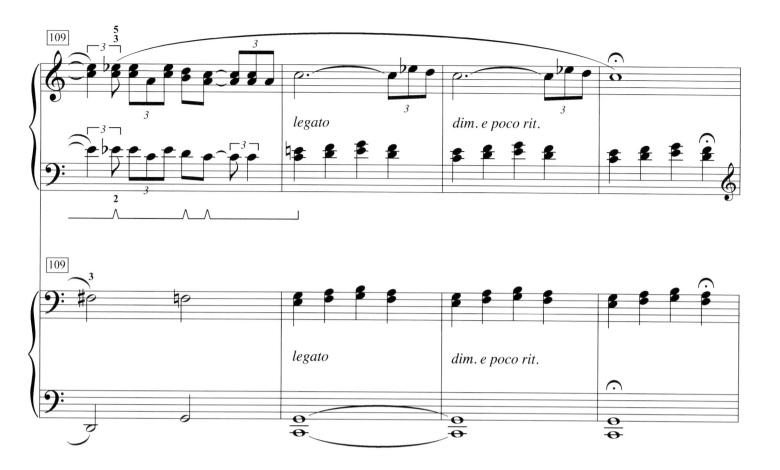

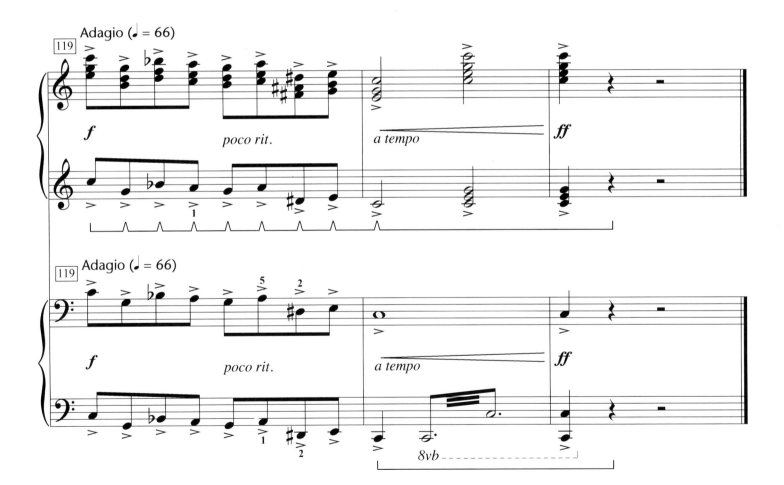